Anne Hotchkis is a university graduate who holds a Bachelor of Science degree (B.Sc.) in Biology, a Bachelor of Education degree (B.Ed.), and a Masters of Education degree (M.Ed.). Her background is in teaching elementary school, and she has written murder mysteries for teens and young adults.

Furthermore, she is married and has two adult sons. Anne enjoys engaging in water activities, listening to music, and going on nature walks. Currently retired, she takes pleasure in traveling and is a deeply spiritual individual, which greatly contributes to her positive outlook on life.

This small book is written for those who live with difficult circumstances in their lives. I would also like to dedicate this book to the memory of my friend, Maitland MacIsaac, who inspired my writing by being my friend. Additionally, I would like to mention my psychiatrist, Dr. Angus Beck, who was there for me as my writing developed and encouraged me to continue telling my story. Finally, I'd like to mention the catalyst for writing this book: my lovely sons, whom I adore.

Anne Hotchkis

You're On Your Own

A Mother's Letters on Life to Her Sons

Austin Macauley Publishers™
LONDON · CAMBRIDGE · NEW YORK · SHARJAH

Copyright © Anne Hotchkis 2024

The right of Anne Hotchkis to be identified as author of this work has been asserted by the author in accordance with sections 77 and 78 of the Copyright, Designs and Patents Act 1988.

All rights reserved. No part of this publication may be reproduced, stored in a retrieval system, or transmitted in any form or by any means, electronic, mechanical, photocopying, recording, or otherwise, without the prior permission of the publishers.

Any person who commits any unauthorised act in relation to this publication may be liable to criminal prosecution and civil claims for damages.

A CIP catalogue record for this title is available from the British Library.

ISBN 9781035843749 (Paperback)
ISBN 9781035843756 (ePub e-book)

www.austinmacauley.com

First Published 2024
Austin Macauley Publishers Ltd®
1 Canada Square
Canary Wharf
London
E14 5AA

Table of Contents

Introduction	9
On Life	11
On Values	13
On Sex	17
On Love	19
On Genetics And Personality Type	21
On Worship	23
On Simplicity	25
On Emotions	28
On The Child Within	30
On Freedom	32
On Complaining	35
On Normalizing	37
On Marriage	39
On Boundaries	41
On Trust	43

On Independence	45
On Raising Children	47
On Tolerance	48
On Education	49
On Finance	51
On Leisure	52
On Loss	53
On Truth	55
On Creativity	56
On Self-Esteem	57
On Health	58
On Social Issues of Our Lives	59
On Kindness	60
On Self	61
On Dementia	62
On Poetry	63
On Being a Grandparent	66

Introduction

It was essential for me to capture the years of growth and development leading me out of the darkness—coming out of an abusive marriage and seven months later being diagnosed with bipolar disorder. The pain was extreme, excruciating, and emotional. I wanted to die, yet I had two young children who were dependent on me. I strongly believed I was the more stable parent, as I had an unshakeable faith in God, so I prayed and prayed for guidance for an intelligent friend who would help carve away the layers of fear, shame, guilt, and marital scars. This friend would also have to be able to give without a financial charge, as I was working in a part-time job and did not have funds to pay for counselling. This person would also have to understand the ups and downs of bipolar illness.

One night when all was quiet in the house, the boys were asleep, and after I said my bedtime prayers and crawled into bed for the night, I had a dream about a local educator. I had not met this man, but his face woke me up at 4:00 a.m. I knew this was the person I had to meet. God chose him while I slept. Early that morning, I phoned his office and made arrangements to meet with him the following week.

The day we met, he asked me why I had come to see him. I said God sent me. That was the beginning of a long friendship lasting over 31 years. He was a candle lighting my way. He showed me what care was all about. I hadn't had that kind of care from someone who would listen deeply as I emptied my soul.

This book contains many heartfelt letters for my sons stemming from the 31 years of friendship I had with this man. Now after counselling with my psychiatrist and conversations with my friend, I am a very peace-filled woman, happily remarried, and living a life of love and respect. The boys are grown, married, and embarking on new territories. This is my gift I give to you with love and adoration, *"You're on Your Own"*.

On Life

Dear Trevor and Tyler,

"What will life out there in the real world, alone and making decisions for myself be like?" you ask.

Truly living—being fully alive—requires a lot of work. Saying you're happy is one thing, yet feeling happiness and peace within yourself requires daily stock-taking of your mental health, physical health, spiritual health, social health. This includes your needs of fun, nutrition, and exercise, creativity, balancing relationships and family demands, your work life, and finding time to pray or meditate, having solitude, juggling the ups and downs, joys, and sorrows of a normal life. Then ask yourself, "What do you have?" You are a happy, loving, caring person. End of story. Isn't there more to life than that?

Life is a journey through time. It is a never-ending, until-death-ending process. Learning to be flexible, accepting disappointments, pains, and unexpected inevitable happenings in stride, and not turning to crutches such as alcoholism or drugs when things get really tough, is hard. Follow your dreams, aspirations, and heart. The doors to the world wait. Wisdom develops with age and experience. I hope

I have offered you a worthy example to calm some of the stormy times ahead.

With you in my prayers,
Mom.

On Values

Dear Trevor and Tyler,

Values are a set of guidelines, code of ethics which establish the boundaries within which you live your life. These values originate from such sources as parents, grandparents, friends, and community of faith. At a particular stage in your life, you will begin to realize your value system is yours alone and does not reflect the values of any one person but becomes a combination of all external sources as well as your own personal inner voice. Standing firm, holding onto your values can sometimes make you feel alienated and lonely. You must ask yourself the question—which is more important, believing in my values or being part of a group? I have always walked the path of life alone; so, I will share some of my earlier writings.

Philosophical Beliefs

1. I believe in the basic values for good living: love, honesty, respect, sharing, and being open to others' perspectives.
2. I believe in maintaining a balanced life to meet my basic needs: physical, belonging, fun, and freedom.

3. Beginning with the family unit, I believe in first of all, being a role model for my family members, but also by fully understanding their age level and developmental stage in life. I respect the basic needs they are trying to fulfil as individuals.
4. In my profession, I believe in the Code of Ethics and maintaining this level of respect with all my clients, patients, students, and staff members.
5. I believe as a member of society from a humanitarian perspective, I must be able to defend my value system.
6. I believe having a faith-based value system is important to give you confidence and stability in your life.
7. I believe organizations such as schools, hospitals, and legal firms need administrators to run them effectively.
8. I believe we live in a complex society with many problems arising from this complexity.
9. I believe many people feel trapped, not knowing where to turn for simplification of these societal complexities.
10. I believe in the power of the *"we"* versus *"I"* theory to broaden my understanding of social issues, complexities of society. Through societal networking look for ways to effect change.

Psychological Beliefs

1. From birth, each and every individual develops into an adult with child, adult, and parental traits.

2. Environmental circumstances play a crucial role in the development of a child's ability to become a mentally healthy adult. Children look up to adult role models.
3. Many adults are affected by scars from their past, choosing to dwell upon negative thought patterns established in their formative years or throughout their life journey.
4. The positive, care-giving emotions in all individuals need fostering, while the parent traits of scepticism, fear, shame, and guilt need to be controlled, thus creating more trusting, open, responsible adults.
5. North American media coverage focuses on the negativity of the world, thus contributing to adults' negative thinking patterns.
6. All humans have the potential for mental wellness with a healthy, positive attitude.

Physical Beliefs

1. Genetics is the cause of many physical disorders.
2. Additionally, there are numerous environmental factors that cause physical problems.
3. A significant number of a physician's caseload of illnesses is attributed to psychological problems that outwardly show physical symptoms.
4. Physicians treat the symptoms based on the physical conditions.

These are standard basic beliefs. Many people believe them, yet when it comes to saying yes, they somehow shy away from the very important responsibility of being a role model for their children. Adults, you are the ones the children in your life look up to. Seek help, ask questions, and strive to become the best role model you can be for your children. As for you, boys, I've tried my best to be the best Mom I could be for you. This is my creed. You will find your own someday.

Believing in you always,
Mom.

On Sex

Dear Trevor and Tyler,

Does having a sexual relationship with someone mean you are in love with that person? I hope you will understand that the act of fornication—having sexual intercourse with another—is satisfying your fleshy, carnal instincts and nothing more. This may sound harsh; however, many people confuse their sexual desires with their image of loving relationships. As you are well aware, I have never had the opportunity to have both of these things—love and sex—from the same person. My strong image of love, with all its passion and romance, combined with a physical relationship, the gentleness of touch in so many beautiful ways, has never been a connection I have had. Please do not misunderstand me. I am not directing you down my life path. I am only writing to you so you can understand me as I am and maybe value some of the differentiations I chose to make in my appreciation of human nature. I spoke with a man about fleshy, carnal instincts and said I valued love and respect more, and he said, "Well that's probably the difference between a man and a woman." My interpretation to that comment was men see sex as more important than women do. Mind you, I'm writing from middle age and at your age my hormones and curiosities about the opposite sex ran rampant.

So, how do you know whether the person you are dating is interested in your personality and character or is just after your body for some sexual pleasure? Many girls in my day and age were brought up with the notion that if you had a sexual relationship with a boy outside of marriage, it was wrong and taboo, and you better marry him. This is a very rigid stance and one that does not fit in today's world. I would like you to become aware of the female need for love and respect versus quick, quick, let's satisfy our sexual desires. There is far more value in developing a long-lasting friendship at the onset of a relationship than becoming lured into the game of "sexual Russian roulette".

Emotions get so muddled and confused once a physical relationship commences. Do I really love her or is it just a physical attraction? Is it the real thing? There can be a great deal of confused emotions, and your rational thinking about the relationship is difficult to sort.

You may think your mother has become too analytical about the mysteries of the opposite sex. Please remember to treat your female companions with the greatest of respect and dignity.

With caution,
Mom.

On Love

Dear boys,

Love is the centre of all living things. It is the heartbeat of life, the breath of life and the motivator that pushes us beyond our human frailties and imperfections, urging to become more alive by creating loving relationships with other people. Love gives to the depths of one's humanity without losing sight of one's own self. Love aspires to godliness.

I once loved so deeply that I lost sight of my own identity. Trying so hard to please another person and, in the process, denying one's own personality and desires, is a concern for anyone developing a lasting relationship. Giving all and having nothing left for yourself is not love; it is control. In a healthy relationship, each person fulfils his/her basic needs and shares his/her life with the other partner. When committing to sharing a life with someone, no one knows whether the relationship will remain healthy. It takes hard work to keep your own identity intact, maintain your friendships, pursue your career, engage in your hobbies and sports activities, share household chores, and accept each other's bad habits, all while creating and growing with another person. Hey, I'm no expert, but I speak from the heart.

As I send you out into the world, I hope and pray for the best life has to offer.

I trust I have not smothered you with too much love. I have seen many children who have been smothered by parents who have burdened their children with needy attachments, preventing them from developing into independent individuals. I hope you have felt my love, support, and care. Just believe in yourself and your own ability to make decisions based on all possible data you have gathered. You will always find people to support your decisions and people to caution you against your views. Detach yourself and see things for what they truly are. Listen to your heart, as there is love at the centre of you. God is love, and god resides within you. When faced with difficulties, turn to your core, and you will find the answer is love.

With heaps of love,
Mom

On Genetics And Personality Type

Dear Trevor and Tyler,

I know you are probably somewhat awed by such a lengthy title for a letter and are apt to wonder what my mother is talking about. Let me clarify your mother's views on these interrelated topics.

Everyone on this planet is born with a particular set of genes. These genes, which hold the information about our biochemical make up and our personality, are found inside the mother's egg cell and the father's sperm cell. When the sperm fertilizes the egg, a genetic code for a new life begins developing. You have both your father's and your mother's good and bad genetic make-up; only each of you has a unique combination which no one else in the world can replicate. Pretty impressive, don't you think? You are the only you in the whole wide world.

As a result of this genetic coding your biochemical makeup, you may inherit some not-so-amazing traits from your parents, particularly when it comes to affecting your choice of activities. For example, if you receive a gene for poor vision, crooked teeth, high blood pressure, diabetes, bipolar disorder, cancer, and so forth, that is the way the combination of genes for your identity happened. Nothing you can do in your power will change that. This is not the end of the story. What you can do is begin to look at ways of changing your attitude and perspective on the world around you. Many people get into blaming behaviours, judging people, throwing fits of anger and despair, feeling helpless and all kinds of negative, unproductive, useless strategies which are more detrimental than advantageous.

I am a firm believer that your life is what your thoughts, words, and actions make it out to be. The power of positive thinking, the assertiveness of positive actions, and acting out of pure love instead of hostility or vengeance are all within your control. Additionally, having a belief in a power greater than yourself is important. If you find yourself reading negative content, it is essential to clear your mind of it and replace it with affirmative and supportive literature. What you expose your brain to is absorbed, processed, and reflected in your actions, attitudes, and words.

The study of personality types is fascinating. By observing people, one can gain insights into their character, almost like looking through a window. The Myers-Briggs Personality Type Indicator is one example of such interesting study in this field, but there are many others as well. While personality type is also genetically based, individuals can learn and work on their weaker areas, improving aspects of their character as they mature and balancing out their preferences. Both of you possess many admirable qualities. Believe in yourself and pursue your dreams.

With love,
Your imperfect mother.

On Worship

Dear Trevor and Tyler,

If I tried to explain the significance and human need to worship in a community of faith to you in words, I think I would fail. Worshiping in any spiritual way towards a higher power, believing you are being guided by this power to fulfil acts of kindness, and making decisions with love at the centre is a lifestyle I have tried to share with you. As you embark on your journey into adulthood, I pray for your inner light, your spirit, to advise you each step of the way. Worshiping with others of similar beliefs offers you a sanctuary and great comfort during difficult times.

I discovered an exquisitely-written quote taped to your grandmother's refrigerator door, and since I couldn't say it any better, I'm including it here for you.

"Worship is the highest act of which man is capable. It not only stretches him beyond all the limits of his finite self to affirm the divine depth of mystery and holiness in the living and eternal God, but it opens him at the deepest level of his being to an act which unites him most realistically with his fellow man."

Samuel H. Miller[1]

Please note Samuel Miller's use of the pronouns, "he" and "his." Your grandmother said I should alter the quote to read "her", in place of the masculine pronouns. However, I didn't think it was ethical to do so, so, it stands intact.

Your spiritual,
Mom

---

1 Samuel H. Miller Quotes from the Journey: Worship quotesfromthejourney.net/worship.htm

On Simplicity

Dear boys,

The world of technology is advancing so rapidly that I've spent the last hour learning how to transfer one file on my computer to a computer disc without losing it on the hard drive. I think there is something wrong with this machine, or am I getting old, or is the world getting too complicated for the limitations of my mind? Take a good look around, and you will see for yourself how bombarded we are with media hype, electronic games, surfing the internet, e-mail, answering machines, and the list goes on and on. Help! I can't keep my body and mind going at the same rate of change that is occurring in my life. Just when I'm at the point of fried brain cells, a wee voice in my head says, *"Get Bored, Get Back to Basics,"* and I begin to try and slow my thoughts down to a speed where the inner self says, "You don't need to understand everything in the entire universe today." Take a few slow breaths, relax, play cards, meditate, read something for a laugh or something uplifting, get some exercise, bake, or, as a last resort do one of those mundane, mindless, chores you've been putting off; i.e., clean out the garbage can, wash the curtains or sort the bookshelves.

Simplicity involves meeting the basic requirements to survive a particularly horrendous day. Did I get enough sleep? Did I wash, brush my hair, brush my teeth, and eat to sustain my body? When pain or misfortune strikes, it is important to have an emergency plan of action. Do nothing! One's physical and emotional energy has its limitations.

When your body or emotions are stressed to the maximum, don't keep driving yourself. Become aware of your personal energy drainers and energy givers. If you are finding at the end of a day or week you are exerting more energy than you are internally gaining, you must discover more sources of rejuvenating the losses of energy you are experiencing.

Everyone needs to find his or her own energy rejuvenators. Physical exercise or playing a sport is one source. Meeting one's own social needs is another. I have had to differentiate between meeting up with a friend for tea and conversation, which is an energy booster for me, and inviting several friends over for a dinner party, which is an energy drainer for me. Extroverts, in general, energize through groups of people, parties, and dances, whereas introverts are fuelled with more solitary, less noisy activities, going for a walk, visiting a friend, or playing cards. Nutrition and spiritual connectedness are other human elements to be monitored carefully when energy has been depleted.

Through all of my darkest and bleakest of times, even when I'd feel no presence of God in my life, I would know to be still and wait. There was some greater power beyond my understanding which was at work. Simplifying one's life to a manageable pace, believing you don't have to know everything today, eating and sleeping well, looking after the essentials, and believing God is there through it all for comfort and support—this is my view of back to basics. Be still, be quiet, and wait. A better day is around the corner.

    Simply,
    Mom

On Emotions

Dear Trevor and Tyler,

Everyone has emotions. To what extent one allows oneself to feel them, experience, wallow in, or relish them depends on the individual's personal awareness and comfort in expressing them. Emotions are both spice and curse of my life. I have loathed, battled with, faced, and surrendered to my emotions. Dynamic, accelerated, seething, rage; desperate, fathomless, pits of self-pity; loneliness, and depression; fanciful, musical, passionate visions of romance; energetic, enthusiastic, gung-ho, task-oriented, love-filled teacher; quiet, gentle, easy going, spiritual, friend; and the myriad of emotions that range in and around the aforementioned comprise the extremes of your mother's emotional self. Emotions the spice and curse of my life.

Those blasted feelings always get in the way of my cool, calm, rational, thinking self. Why can't I lasso them up, compartmentalize them, and forge bravely into new territory with a serene, tranquil expression. Many people manage to suppress unwanted emotions or have learned behaviours which allow them to express their emotions in analytical, balanced, and cognitive ways. Oh, what a wistful dream. Reactive is my middle name. In the heat of anger, I have learned to remove myself from the scene and to chill out to regain my composure from a frazzled, shaken state. Fortunately, anger does not frequently cast its monstrous shadow in our house. Yet, as you age, your ego seeks a voice of its own, and I'm beginning to hear the echoes of my own and your father's voice in you.

Let's browse the more popular, positive emotions of compassion, empathy, gentleness, thoughtfulness, passion, enthusiasm, excitement, and happiness. This is a brief list of the many positive, caring emotions we experience. You will need to learn and expand your own emotional repertoire. I have always believed we should dwell on the positive, focus on it, savour it, embellish it; somehow positive thoughts we are working so hard to keep in the forefront of our mind begin to seep into our subconscious, permeating our being with love, peace, and serenity. It is a tactic I use to overcome the ugly.

You are from a reactive family. Both of you have weathered many emotional mountains and valleys. Continue to strive to share your feelings in healthy, non-harmful ways.

With love,
Mother.

On the Child Within

Dear children,

The secret of everlasting youth is not found in the Fountain of Youth or at the end of the rainbow, nor is it a difficult soul-searching endeavour. It is the simplest of all our life's gifts. The requirement is that you don't kill the child within, and don't suppress it when it wants to come out to play. All of us through our adult, parent, and child perceptions, far too often neglect the childlike, fun-filling needs by adult reasoning, saying that such behaviour is childish. It is not.

Don't tell me you've never wanted to walk backwards through a field so people wouldn't know which direction you were traveling, catch a grasshopper and keep him for a pet, link arms and skip down the street singing your favourite tune, run outside with a cake of soap to shower in the summer rain, climb a tree, swing a swing up to touch the sky, carve your initials in a rock to leave your mark, or make snow angels on a crisp, winter day.

All of us have, if not many, some happy childhood memories and, if you don't, begin imagining some fanciful ones for yourself.

Here and now, today, stop bypassing life, missing the sweet fundamental joys, beauties, laughter, excitement, and elements of surprise that a child so dearly loves. Imprint in your mind a child's excitement on Christmas morning, the warmth of a child's loving hug, the simple faith and trust that children have in the adults in their life. We can learn a lot about staying young forever. All we have to do is disentangle the complicated network of falsely-created barriers we've built to protect ourselves. These walls isolate us, not only from the evils of the world, but from the purest, happiest, most-treasured moments we can possibly enjoy.

So today, reflect upon you, the child, and if you haven't been having enough fun lately, remind yourself to be more child-like. These child-like experiences will keep you young forever.

Your childhood counsellor,
Mom.

On Freedom

Dear Trevor and Tyler,

Everything worth having in this world has a price tag on it. What I mean is you must sacrifice certain pictures in your head of what you think you want and need to fulfil the more pressing visions you have for yourself. When your father and I separated, I gave up the picture of having a loving, caring relationship with a man and replaced it with being the best mother, teacher, most loving person I could be. In truth, there were no suitable men knocking at my door during these years. The reality was I could not compromise my images of devoted, dedicated mother with what a man in my life would do to our family unit. It was a conflict in my mind but freedom has a price. Everything has a price.

Freedom means letting go of control, all control, and total control. The minute you realize you have done this then you can start taking back controls that you choose for yourself. I gave up so many pictures of what other people thought I should be and then thought about what I want to be for myself, for you boys, for a quality of life that I can choose for us as a family.

I know life has not always been easy for you. When bad luck, painful events, or crisis occurs in our lives, we are thrown off balance emotionally, mentally, physically, and sometimes socially. When we begin to accept the new life change, whether it is a death, divorce, illness, we begin to normalize our lives once again. We create a new equilibrium. Many people are so scarred by their painful journey through life that they take on negative thinking patterns and a blaming-the-world attitude.

You are free—free to make decisions for yourself, free to develop the quality of life you choose for yourself. We have the God-given right to feel freedom, whether we are married or not. I have spoken with many people who are having difficult times in relationships. I wish to offer these people comfort and realization that their children will be the ones to suffer if an unhealthy relationship continues. Nevertheless, many factors come into play when one makes a major decision such as I did with a separation. The issues are a complex web of interwoven lives which are unique for each particular situation. No one can tell another person what is the best option. This decision must come from the persons involved.

You may ask my perceptions on any particular topic, but remember, I am only your loving mother. I cannot make the decisions for you. You will have to take ownership of the choices you make and not blame anyone else for a good or bad choice. We all make mistakes. How else would we learn if we did not grow through the pain into a new more holy place?

Life is a continuous, ongoing process. We take two steps forward and one step back, and then we take one step forward and two steps back. We are living a dance and are dancing around the floor of our creation.

Independently yours,

Mom

On Complaining

Dear Trevor and Tyler,

Today's lesson is on complaining. Doesn't everyone like to complain to a listening ear? I've got a headache, I've got lower back problems, I'm constipated, I don't have enough money, there are not enough hours in the day. If we can find a compassionate ear, we've found a dumping ground for our woes.

It is a fact of life that we need a healthy support system of friends and family to help us through life's trials and tribulations. Letting one's hair down with these people offers one emotional support and comfort when the unfortunate events of life afflict us. However, complaining as a steady diet can strain your truest loving relationships and infest your mind causing a terrible habit-forming negative in your personality.

Beware, or, I should say, be conscious of the force of negative thinking. Don't allow your life to be controlled by its power. Life, being fully human, means it is commonplace for us to share our troubles with a friend. Friends are a valuable and treasured gift, so share with them and be appreciative of them. Your family does not want to be bombarded by negative thoughts. So where should you turn when you've exhausted your list of friends and family with your lamenting?

There is only one true source of strength in your life. It is the path of the truth which no other human being can offer you. It is the path which comes from inner meditation and prayer. Calming one's self down to reach one's centre, finding peace, spirituality in love, not knowing the answers to all of life's questions, and yet knowing that's okay because no one has all the answers, is surrender. Surrender to God. Unconditional surrender is faith.

Be positive,
Mom.

On Normalizing

Dear Boys,

Tragedy strikes! It does not matter who you are or what job you have; bad luck and hard times are inevitable. How you cope with death of a loved one, job layoffs, divorce, unfaithfulness in a relationship, alcoholism, illness, financial burdens are the key to living a successful, enriched and rewarding life. I'm the last person in the world to say all of the above are easy breaks. They are painful life occurrences.

When I went through my divorce and then was diagnosed with my illness only a few months after the marriage break-up I thought I was going to die. The pain was excruciating. I can go back there in my mind and replay vivid scenarios which cause me to burst into tears. My friend, who lost his son to cancer, lived each day with his son's face in front of him. I can cite numerous situations in family members' lives and friends' lives which are equally as pain stricken. Your grandmother doesn't even want to talk about her childhood years, as they are too painful for her to discuss.

Normalizing. What is normalizing? Life is hard. This is a well-documented fact. Normalizing is seizing the pain, transforming it through a metamorphic change within you, adapting, moulding, and shaping yourself to face it head on, educating yourself about your circumstances and then relearning how to live all over again as your new self. Normalizing is taking a difficult life episode and making it normal. Everyone must learn to take the tough breaks in stride. Regaining one's balance and then living according to the parameters you establish for yourself is normalizing. Healthy people bounce back. Stay healthy.

    Healthy and Normal,
    Mom

On Marriage

Dear sons,

The time has come for me to set you free, to join your partner in marriage, and create a life of your own together. That doesn't mean I won't be around if you are inclined to ask for my opinion; however, I know my place, and I am no longer going to smother you with motherly love. What is marriage? Marriage is facing the ups and downs of life with a loving companion. It is not control. It is not submissiveness. It is respect and love for each other in all walks of life. It is giving of yourself, putting your spouse first and foremost when it comes to decision-making. It is being free to become the creation God intended you to be within the societal structure of the bonds of marriage. It is living the straight and narrow path of goodness and godliness with thoughts of kindness and thoughtfulness towards your spouse.

Both of you, as you grow, will seek your past to make sense of your lives. Your mother and father did only what we thought was right for you. We've made mistakes, but hey, we are not perfect. Please don't blame your parents. We did what we could do. Now I'm saying to you and your bride, "*You're on Your Own*".

Best wishes always,
    Mom

On Boundaries

Dear sons,

I've been reminiscing about your childhood and smiling over all the trials and tribulations I felt as a single parent, creating and developing the boundaries I wanted you to have as you grew up. Little did I know that the boundaries I established would be tested and stretched to the limit as you entered adolescence.

What were the boundaries I desperately wanted to develop in you? At age three, I taught you to look both ways before you crossed the street, always stay buckled in your seatbelt when going in the car, say grace before a meal and chew your food well.

There were many other wishful boundaries I tried to create but my attempts for you to pick up after yourselves never really came to fruition, as I personally struggled with a lack of organizational skills. Thus, we had a less-than-tidy house and car, but more of a special, loving atmosphere together except for the brotherly battles you had with each other. At these occurrences I'd unsuccessfully try to mediate between the two of you. Unsolved battles sent me to avoid the conflict by retreating to another quiet room.

My memories reject the torture and pain you gave to each other, and now that you are adults, I am overjoyed that there are no more arguments. My future dream is that your children will be blessed and that you will find more creative ways of childhood management.

Letting go…
Mom

On Trust

Hello again guys,

Trust is a virtue of faith in others. I always had faith and trust in you two. I wanted to offer you a sincere, quiet, home life, but it wasn't that way. I wanted to be a great listener, but I wasn't. I wanted to purify my soul and let my purity rub off on you but it didn't work that way. My flaws were reflected in the personalities created by our lives together. Trust accepts all attributes of another character, good and bad. Trust is sacred: believing in another's goodness and godliness, sharing each other's stories, and keeping their stories in your confidence. Backbiting and gossiping about others' trusted loyalties is evil, taboo, and downright insensitive.

Be a confidant with your family and friends. Be a role model of trustfulness.

"Trust in the Lord with all thine heart and lean not on thy own understanding."

The Bible[2]

"Be patient under all conditions, and place your whole trust and confidence in God."

---

[2] Proverbs 3:5 King James Version of the Holy Bible

Baha'u'llah[3]

With all my trust,
Mom

---

[3] Baha'u'llah, Gleanings from the Writings of Baha'u'llah, Chapter CXXXVI p.295

On Independence

Dear young men,

Today's world is full of scary, unsafe, fearful events. They are too numerous to mention. However, I did not dwell on the negatives of the world. As you grew, I focused on all the sunshine values, working very hard to overcome our past pain.

Independence occurred when you left home, got married, and severed your childhood ties, with your newfound status as a married man. You now share your personal adult wisdom and knowledge with your wife and friends. Making decisions for yourself, despite what others think you should or shouldn't do, make you an independent thinker.

I encouraged education, you chose your own path.

Sharing adult to adult with you individually has been a new experience for me, and at times, I just want to hold you in my arms again. Detachment and acceptance that I already completed my job and have sent you forth into the world are important. I remind you to keep a positive attitude, not overreact, and keeping your emotions in check are all ways to live in the adult world.

Independently yours,
Mom

On Raising Children

Dear Trevor and Tyler,

There are many books on how to raise children, but I didn't want to read another author's viewpoint, as I had my own childhood memories of creativity, music, sports, etc. that I wanted to instil in you. Plus, I wanted you to feel positive, not fearful about life, and I wanted to forget the hardships of your lives.

There are different stages of development, from infancy to adulthood. Each stage gives a child more and more freedom until adolescence when parents struggle with the letting go syndrome to the overprotective syndrome. From my experience the Letting Go Syndrome paid off big time as I gave you freedom to be independent.

Paranoia and worry about what others think of you are dangerous negatives. Keep a stiff upper lip, follow kindness, gentleness, and all the caring virtues, and your lives will be joy-filled and peaceful.

Love,
Mom

On Tolerance

Dear sons,

He makes me so mad. Why did she blame me? That's not fair. Tolerance.

Tolerance and patience go hand in hand. Avoiding conflicts, talking through issues, discussing adult-to-adult your differences of opinions, showing respect and being sensitive to other people's feelings go a long way toward building tolerance on the job and in your home life.

I grew up terrified of conflict, so much that I'd deny and suppress my own opinions. It's important to know when and how to express yourselves in healthy, compassionate ways. Don't be blunt or harsh; be pleasant and positive. Be diplomatic in the workplace and take that attribute home.

I care so much about your warm, cosy, loving home lives that I want your families to grow in peaceful surroundings.

Love,
Mom

On Education

Dear Trevor and Tyler,

I wish for you to become lifelong learners. Create and educate all aspects of yourselves. Think about becoming more selfless and enrich your lives with a strong powerful, faith in God. This will help shape your character. University education was important to me, and I'm glad both of you graduated in your respective fields of study. However, being a university graduate doesn't mean you stop learning. Delve into projects that interest you and grow through the learning process. It could be anything from making bread to producing a musical. Happiness in life requires daily thoughts of where you want to grow and then begin taking steps towards your goals.

When it comes to spiritual growth, take a deep inner look at personality quirks that you wish to change. It is easier to pick out the quirks of your partner than it is to work on your own flaws. Wisdom and knowledge arrive when you've purified your mind, heart, and soul.

Grow, learn, develop, adapt, adjust, mould, educate for life.

Your life-long learner,
Mom

On Finance

Dear sons,

Live within your means. Try to stay out of debt. Of course, this doesn't mean you can't have a mortgage. Pay off student loans. Save for a holiday. These are all words of advice. I shall continue: don't spend what you don't have, avoid overuse of credit cards; be careful. Save for a rainy day.

If you run into financial trouble, get a financial advisor. Learn how to budget. Avoid addictive habits such as drinking, smoking, and gambling. Be moderate.

Living a good quality of life requires you to have a solid financial background.

Many people live with stressful financial burdens. I hope you can find a contented, low-stress, financially-stable life.

Love,
Mom

On Leisure

Dear sons,

How does one measure leisure time? There are many ways to recover from an extraordinary difficult work week, month, or year. Life is like a puzzle trying to fit all the pieces together. Today, I wish to share more pleasant kinds of activities—leisure.

Travel, sports, canoeing, camping, the arts, music, drama, musicals, reading, games, socializing, friendship, joining clubs, nature hikes, going to the beach, and so on. Whatever you decide for yourselves as fun, you can chalk it up to leisure activities. Do you remember your first airplane ride? Your trip to Montreal? The snow forts in the backyard? The campfires on the beach? The forts on the bank? Both of you were very creative in your leisure time.

Sports, hockey, judo, swimming? If you ever get bored with life, think of a new leisure activity and integrate it into your family. Remember, life is what your thoughts, feelings and actions make it. Be happy and have fun.

Your fun-filled,
Mom

On Loss

Dear Trevor and Tyler,

Grief over lost loved ones is an energy-draining and emotional time in your life. It can be a black cloud hanging over your head, and depending on your relationship with the deceased, you may remain living with a hole in your heart for the rest of your life. You have experienced loss of a pet and loss of grandparents. I grieved the loss of our pet dog and have wonderful fond memories of her, but the time came when she was too old and too crippled with arthritis to keep her alive. Having her put down was the humane thing to do. You were young when I made this decision, and I didn't want to tell the truth about her end of life. She was a wonderful addition to our family.

Memories are individual impressions we have of the people we have lost, and the age you were when you lost your grandparents affects the pain you feel. I had a friend whose pain lived with him daily as he lost his only son in the early 1990s. That was 30 years ago. One must learn to relive one's life putting the grief into a little box in one's brain and only opening it to have a look, but not to become overwhelmed and burdened so much that it inhibits living a full and happy life. Remember to give the loss up to God and pray for peace. After all, the person you have lost is in heaven and in a much better place than you or me. Believe in heaven. It is comforting.

    Your healed,
    Mom

On Truth

Dear young men,

What is the truth? Whose truth is true? We all have perceptions based on experience that led us to believe our perception is the truth. Let me share with you the importance of you and your wife agreeing on a very significant scenario, raising children. Sometimes you have to agree to disagree but make a fully-unified front for the sake of the family. Unity in the family is a priority. If your child plays one-against-the-other games as he/she get older, your family becomes a battle zone. It is important to consult with your wife and make the children understand you and your wife will not tolerate little, white lies. Be honest with each other and keep the family running smoothly. I will continue to pray for a happy, unified family even as the sea of life is not always smooth sailing.

Good luck,
Mom

On Creativity

Dear sons,

Creativity and finding pleasure in making something new with your hands, feet, or mouth are wonderful ways to express your gifts from God. Being creative is adventurous, whether it is cooking, sewing, writing, building, fixing up an old item and making it like new. Painting, drawing, and many other ways of self-expression give you another dimension to life. I have seen both of you develop many forms of creativity. I like to write poetry, mysteries, experiment with cooking, and sometimes get involved in musical groups. I have seen you, Trevor, building furniture, and you, Tyler, creating new inventions. Both of you show different ways of self-expression, so have fun creating in your own individual ways.

Have fun,
Mom

On Self-Esteem

Dear sons,

Wellness and life-management skills all contribute to self-esteem. There was a time when I had no self-esteem, living under the control of my first husband. It took me a very long time to overcome this negative influence in my life but even more so to overcome the bipolar label I received as a result of my separation. I look back over the years and see where I was and how far I've come, and feel pretty fine about myself and my new marriage. I continue to be sensitive to harsh words a friend might dump on me or to misinterpretation by persons in authority. Nevertheless, I am much quicker to get over it and don't wallow any more in unhealthy ways. I am learning to stand up for myself, becoming more detached emotionally from situations, and fending for myself without feelings arising out of control. Hey, I'm beginning to like the person I have become.

Love,
Mom

On Health

Dear guys,

Take care of your body physically, mentally, and spiritually. I have decided to do a little spiel, so here goes: keep your body clean, brush your teeth after every meal, eat healthy foods, reduce fats, sodium; eat lots of green vegetables. Veggies and fruit give vitamins and minerals to your body; protein repairs cells in the body; and carbs give you energy. Drink lots of water, cut down on sugars, get enough sleep, try to avoid too much processed food, manage your stress, find ways to exercise, and rest. Balance exercise and rest; don't be a workaholic.

Enjoy life,
Mom

On Social Issues of Our Lives

Dear Trevor and Tyler,

It is with great love for you that I wish to make a list of social problems our lives are exposed to on a regular basis. We can only extend our selves so far to help individuals we come in contact through personal experience or through community, national, or world organizations. There are many organizations out there working to create a better life for others. Please ponder the list. You may agree or disagree with any number of them, so here goes: alcoholism, gambling, drug abuse, smoking, prostitution, rape, violence, family abuse, bullying, abortion, eating disorders—obesity, anorexia, bulimia—divorce, homelessness, incest, gang behaviour, pornography, poverty, poor self-image, suicide or attempted suicide, illiteracy, lack of education, lack of family values, sexual deviation, prejudice, and discrimination.

Many countries of the world have inequality of men and women, which is also a world problem. Be prepared to extend help to others without creating too much stress on your health and the health of your family.

With care,
Mom

On Kindness

Dear Trevor and Tyler,

There are many things in hindsight that I wished I had taught you. Hopefully, you've already learned the value of kindness. As youth, you were not very kind to each other and the house appeared in chaos. Now, though, as you've married and are sharing your life with your wife, let me refresh your memory of kindness, thoughtfulness. Give of yourself without thinking you are measuring how kind you are by doing the thoughtful things for those around you. Be in touch with your gentle side and put others first in your life. Don't take each other for granted. Share experiences as two adult men, avoid harsh words, and respect each other's ideas and thoughts as individuals in order to help keep family ties together. Be encouraging, and don't talk negatively about people behind their backs. Use language to inspire others to fulfil their full potential. Speak respectfully using loving words, in other words, "to thine own self be true" but do it diplomatically. You have both shown me examples of kindness. Keep it up.

With kindness,
Mom

On Self

Dear guys,

The word "self" has two meanings: 1) One is self, the identity of the individual created by God. This is the self that is mentioned in such passages as "he hath known God who hath known himself"[4]... 2) The other self is the ego, the dark, animalistic aspect each one of us has, the lower nature that can develop into a monster of selfishness, brutality, lust and so on. It is this self we must struggle against, or this side of our nature, in order to free the spirit within us and help it to attain perfection. It is in writing these letters that I am freeing my spirit to share with you my identity created by God.

Prayerfully,
Mom

---

[4] Baha'u'llah, Gleanings from the Writings of Baha'u'llah Chapter XC p. 177

On Dementia

Dear Trevor and Tyler,

This is a sad reality of our family, as you've seen your grandmother deteriorate right before your eyes with dementia. She was a high-energy, active, positive, enthusiastic care giver, alpine skier, artist, extroverted woman, who deteriorated on a downward slope because of memory loss and became a helpless nursing home resident. How things have changed so dramatically. I tried to call her every day. Surprisingly, I found that her memory for music and songs we which we sang since I was a child was stored in a part of her brain that I could tap into, and the two of us sang daily with each other. This was the only way I could reach her at this stage of her life.

I know neither one of you has memorized songs, and I don't want to be a burden on you should I end up like Mom, so please don't keep me alive if my brain has gone. I agree with doctor-assisted death. Please let me go.

Let me go,
Mom

On Poetry

Dear sons,

You have both seen some of my poetry, been at my book launches, and know that poetry is my way of self-expression. Writing these letters to you has been a cathartic liberation. It has been both my life leisure and work to enrich your lives with my thoughts and philosophy through poetry. Maybe not all of it is great poetry, but at times I feel compelled to write free-flowing words on paper to represent my soul and spirit.

So here is one of the last poems I've written this year:

Faith
God chose me to lead the people,
One by one,
From an emotional perspective,
To a new found faith and freedom.

My soul spoke these words
I did not understand
All of them
Until after many years,
A Baha'i man came into my life.

A new found faith
The Baha'i Faith
My Christian beliefs were challenged.
I studied Ruhi books.
Became friends with other Baha'is.
Became one of them.

Progressive revelation
World religions, one and all,
Diversity and unity
Amongst cultures and neighbors.

Community
Religions
Freedom to pick and choose
Personal beliefs.

I am a spiritual being.
I strive to be more God-like.
I envelop the words of poets,
philosophers, religious leaders,
And scientists.

One by one, I share love
with individuals
on my path
creating new friends.
Keeping those who

have altered my life.
Love always,
Mom

On Being a Grandparent

Dear fathers,

You've made it to the next generation. You are now fathers, and I am a grandmother. It seems like I've been writing letters for a very long time. It was over 25 years since it all began. There are now three granddaughters in our family.

I look into your eyes and see that the course of letter writing has made you lovely, handsome fathers, independent and striving to live fully healthy lives. I see your girls so precious, so beautiful, so real. I have come full circle in my feelings. I am overjoyed, enraptured, enthralled with this stage of my life. I am happy that your families are so delightful. I love your wives, your children, and both of you. I see that, "your own your own," and I can continue to create activities that involve the extension of our family—birthdays, family gatherings, special days, and meals. I think I'm going to cry, I'm so happy. This is the end of this book but only the beginning of grandparenthood.

Love you one and all,
Mom

Made in the USA
Monee, IL
03 May 2026

49437838R00037